ENOUGH PEACE AND QUIET FOR A FULL DAY

REST STOPS *for* BUSY MOMS

ENOUGH PEACE AND QUIET FOR A FULL DAY

REST STOPS
for
BUSY
MOMS

WRITTEN AND COMPILED BY

SUSAN TITUS OSBORN

Nashville,
Tennessee

REST STOPS FOR BUSY MOMS
Copyright © 2003 by Susan Titus Osborn
All Rights Reserved

Broadman & Holman Publishers, Nashville, Tennessee
ISBN 0-8054-2667-1

Dewey Decimal Classification: 242.643
Subject Heading: Mothers/Women/Devotional Literature

All Scripture verses are taken from the Holman Christian Standard Bible®
Copyright © 1999, 2000, 2001, 2002, 2003 by Holman Bible Publishers.

Caseside printed in the United States. Text printed and bound in Mexico.
2 3 4 06 05 04 03

Contents

Dedication

To
Michele Osborn and Robyn Johnson,
my sweet daughters by marriage.

My ten precious grandkids in these two families
give these two women the right to
the title "Busy Mom."

Introduction

Today we live in a busy world of minute breakfasts, fast-food lunches, microwaveable dinners, and instant coffee and tea. Although we have more timesaving devices than the women of past generations, moms today are working more hours than ever before. Consequently, we find ourselves with less free time. It seems that the more we try to do, the more that remains undone.

We expect knowledge and information to come instantaneously, too, in our electronic age of televisions, videos, computers, and cellular phones. These electronic wonders are always waiting at our fingertips. Consequently, we never escape from them. Is it possible to find quality time to spend with those we love as well as quiet time to spend with God in the midst of this frantic activity? And how do we find time to nurture ourselves?

Today's women are working part-time or full-time outside the home while the housework builds up and begs to be done.

Plus, our children are involved in more and more activities. We are forever rushing them to practices and games and recitals for baseball, soccer, dance, football, swimming, T-ball, piano, softball, ballet, karate, and hockey. Not only do we feel driven by all that needs to be done, but also we are always driving. These things are important and should not be neglected, but we don't get much accomplished on our "to do" lists while sitting behind the steering wheels of our cars. We have to be careful not to become slaves to the "doing" and neglect the "being" of our inner selves.

As our children grow and become more independent, we are able to reclaim some of our lost time. Yet new challenges and different problems arise. Peer pressure can be overwhelming for teenagers, often resulting in a battle of wills between parents and offspring. Our teens are involved in fighting temptations not even thought of when we were growing up. Learning to cope with all of this pressure can prove tremendously challenging to us, as well as to our kids.

Spouses, bosses, friends, as well as church and community commitments also make demands on our time, and they take their toll. Many of us spend our entire lives doing for others—trying to please everyone we know. This proves to be an impossible task, and we run ourselves ragged until we reach a point where we are not enjoying anything we do at all.

This does not mean, however, that we should totally ignore the needs of others. Jesus tells us in Matthew 22:39 to love our neighbor as ourselves. We show love for others by giving them our time, listening to them, encouraging them, and showing compassion. Yet all this must be done with balance. Achieving a good balance in our lives can be difficult to accomplish. It's something we need to reevaluate constantly.

Yet we often forget the second part of that commandment: to love . . . as ourselves. If we are attempting to love our neighbors, friends, relatives, and coworkers at the expense of ourselves, we have not followed God's second commandment. And we may soon experience burnout.

Jesus also said, "Come to Me, all you who are weary and burdened, and I will give you rest. Take My yoke upon you and learn from Me, because I am gentle and humble in heart, and you will find rest for your souls. For My yoke is easy and My burden is light" (Matthew 11:28-30).

God has promised us that a relationship with Him will change meaningless, wearisome toil into spiritual productivity and purpose. This book is designed to help you find "rest stops" in Him that will refresh and rejuvenate you.

Slowly steep yourself a cup of tea and carry it to your favorite recliner. Put your head back and your feet up. Relax and enjoy these *Rest Stops for Busy Moms*.

Part One
SHARING WITH FRIENDS

Special friends listen when we need to talk. They are patient while we pour out our hearts to them. They feel our pain, and our relationships grow as a result of that sharing. Sometimes they don't have to say a word, but at other times we find their wisdom invaluable. Special friends are there during the difficult times of our lives, and they are also there in our good times, laughing with us and sharing our special moments. Special friendships last for a lifetime.

A friend loves at all times, and a brother is born for a difficult time.

—PROVERBS 17:17

Who AM I?

I sat down at the kitchen table with a cup of tea and sighed. My neighbor, Helen, had come over for a few minutes while our preschoolers played in the backyard.

"Helen, I'm really struggling with my identity," I said, pouring my heart out to my best friend. "At the preschool, I'm known as Mike's mom. When my husband and I go out socially, people call me 'Dick's wife.' Doesn't anybody realize I have a name?"

"Of course they do, Susan," she replied.

"I feel like my whole life is wrapped up in doing things for my husband and kids. I wonder if I'm doing anything truly worthwhile."

Helen placed her hand on mine. "You sound frustrated."

"I love my family. It just seems that everything I do is mundane and nonproductive. I clean the house, and ten minutes after the boys come in, it looks like a cyclone hit it."

"I know. I feel the same way," said Helen. "When I cook a special gourmet meal, the family wolfs it down in ten minutes without saying a word."

"That beats having someone say, 'Yuck! I don't like it. What is this?'" I laughed halfheartedly.

"Yeah. *'Eww, this looks funny. Can't we have hot dogs?'*" mimicked Helen.

We looked at each other and burst out laughing.

Then on a more serious note, Helen said, "But, you know, we can't judge our own successes or failures by how our families react to our cooking and cleaning."

"I realize that, but sometimes it's hard to find a guideline to see if what we are doing is worthwhile."

Helen waited for a moment and chose her words carefully. "Our guideline needs to come from God. Does He think we are involved in worthwhile activities? A good question to ask ourselves is, 'Is what I'm doing pleasing to Him?'"

"I see what you are saying!" I said, feeling a little better. "We need to look beyond the mundane chores that are never-ending and focus on God and who He created us to be."

"Yes. And remember, we aren't just cleaning muddy hands and faces. We are building lives, molding our little ones to be all they can be for Him, too."

—*Susan Titus Osborn*

With every deed you are sowing a seed, though the harvest you may not see.

—ELLA WHEELER WILCOX

Half the Fun
IS GETTING THERE

It never crossed our minds that we were doing something outrageous. Although it was summer vacation, both our husbands had to work. Yet Annette, pregnant and showing, and I with my hurt knee decided to take our kids and get away. With five children under the age of seven, we knew our trip would not be lacking adventure.

We packed the van carefully. With sleeping bags, five squirt guns, junk food, and the latest chick flick that had hit the market, we headed toward the mountains. Even with *Veggie Tales* playing in the background, it wasn't long until our crew became restless.

"He's touching me!"

"He *has* to touch you, we're packed in here like sardines," I replied.

"How long until we get there?"

"Hey, everybody," Annette said in her teacher voice. "Remember, half the fun is getting there!"

A couple of hours later, we rounded the mountain and soon stood on the doorsteps of Oakhaven, my parents' mountain home.

"Who's got the key?" one of the kids hollered.

The key! Oh no! In the midst of packing the van, I had set the key down on my kitchen counter. I had forgotten it!

Immediately I said a quick prayer. Then grabbing Annette's arm, I whispered in her ear, "Remember how you said 'half the fun is getting there'? Well, we're not even inside yet, and the key is at home on my kitchen counter!"

A friend is a gift you give yourself.

—ROBERT LOUIS STEVENSON

16

Quickly turning our situation into a game, Annette, the kids, and I began rattling all the doors and checking all the windows for a way inside.

"Look here!" Annette shouted. "The kitchen window above the sink doesn't have a safety lock. Janet, if you hoist me up, I think I can open the window and crawl through."

"You can *what*? You're pregnant!"

"Well, you can't do it. You've got a bad knee."

Before I knew it, all five kids stood cheering, watching Annette crawl though the window while I braced her. As Annette's feet disappeared from sight, one of her kids shouted, "Mom, remember that half the fun is getting there!"

We had a great time during our vacation at Oakhaven. The kids laughed, played, hiked, and even learned to whistle through an acorn. Annette and I found the time to talk like schoolgirls, and late one night when the kids were tucked in bed, we curled up and watched our chick flick.

Looking back to the days when Annette and I so daringly headed for the mountains with our little brood, we both smile. Now we know for certain that half the fun of motherhood is sharing it with a friend.

—*Janet Lynn Mitchell*

Operation
ENDURING SLEEP

We call it "Operation Enduring Sleep." My husband and I, the two-member coalition in this war on sleep deprivation, take our assignment very seriously. The mission: to transfer our sleeping toddler, Jordan, from his car seat to his bed without waking him.

After we deploy ourselves, our first step is to unhook the buckle on his restraining device. Jordan sighs, and we freeze. Our lips purse, our foreheads crease, and we both wonder if we'll make it.

After unhooking our little soldier, we give silent instructions to one another. Carey mouths, "You get him. I'll get the door." I nod in agreement.

Holding my breath, I slip Jordan's car seat strap over his head. So far, so good. Now the most dangerous part: the hoist. I carefully bring my son's heavy arms up over my shoulders, wrap one arm around his waist, and cover his head. I don't want to bump it on the car door and accidentally end the operation.

My brave husband holds the door for me and I walk past him. Trooper that he is, Carey has already been on a stealth mission in our son's bedroom. We both know that any miscalculation or stumble on my part would prove fatal to our plan, so Carey has pulled the bedcovers back, darkened the room, and conducted a ground search for stray objects in Jordan's room.

As I reach the target, Jordan stirs a bit. I hesitate, recalculate, and start humming a lullaby. Carey follows stealthily behind me, whispering encouragement. "Almost there," he says.

Fatigue is the best pillow.

—BENJAMIN FRANKLIN

Then ever so gently I place Jordan on his bed, take off his shoes, and cover his body with a blanket. I tiptoe away, giving Carey the thumbs-up sign. Mission accomplished.

"Mommy?" I hear a young, soft voice. My heart starts to race. *No,* I think. *We've come too far to fail now! I need my sleep, too!* I slowly tiptoe away, ignore my child, and hope he's not really awake.

"Mommy!" Jordan cries, louder this time. I grimace at Carey. He shrugs, and I turn back around. Our son is sitting up in bed, rubbing his eyes. "I'm not tired anymore."

"You need more rest," I whisper. "Go back to sleep."

Jordan hops off his bed, runs to my side, and raises his arms. "I want to hold you!" he says.

I reach down and scoop my son into my arms. And so the mission is aborted. Jordan knows my weak spots, and he isn't afraid to exploit them.

After an extended hug, I place him on the floor. He immediately runs over to his dad. Carey lifts him high in the air and gives him a bear hug. Finally, after two bedtime stories and a glass of water, Jordan settles down.

As Carey and I tiptoe out of the room hand-in-hand, I turn and look at my sleeping child. I say a silent prayer of thankfulness for my active toddler and for the special man beside me, my husband and best friend.

—*Dena J. Dyer*

Part Two
UNEXPECTED BLESSINGS

Often the most memorable moments of our lives are found during the most surprising times. These unexpected blessings can come in any form: a bouquet of dandelions presented to us by a child, a kind word from a friend over a soothing cup of tea, or a relaxing moment in a hot tub filled with bubbles. The important thing is to recognize the moment, to relax and enjoy it, and accept it as a little gift from God.

She opens her mouth with wisdom,
and loving instruction is on her tongue.
She watches over the activities
of her household and is never
idle. Her sons rise up and
call her blessed.

—PROVERBS 31:26–28

Prom
NIGHT

Obstacles are those frightful things you see when you take your eyes off your goal. —HENRY FORD

"I don't have much money to give you to spend for the prom," I said to my younger son, Mike, sadness filling my voice. I had prayed that God would somehow make this special occasion possible for my son, but I didn't see how. As a single mom with myself and another son in college, I could only stretch my finances so far.

"I know, Mom," replied Mike, "but could you buy the flowers?" He stood in the kitchen, looking at me expectantly.

"I guess I can handle that," I said. In the back of my mind I was wondering where he would get the money for all the other things: a tuxedo, a limousine, prom tickets, pictures, dinner.

Prom night had become such an outrageously expensive extravaganza for high school kids. Yet I didn't want my son to miss this special event.

One morning about a week before the prom, Mike came downstairs before school . . . dressed in a tuxedo! "Are you wearing that to school?" I asked, too sleepy to even ask where the thing came from.

"BJ's Formal Wear will give me a tux for the prom for free if I wear one to school for three days and hand out their business cards," he announced confidently. "I'm supposed to get all my friends to rent their tuxes there."

I realized what a sacrifice wearing that tight shirt and bow tie was for my casual son who balked at even wearing a coat and tie. "That's great, Mike!" I managed to blurt out.

"What are you doing for dinner on prom night?" I asked, deciding to voice a few of my concerns.

"Well, I meant to say something about that, Mom. Would it be okay if I invited Sandy over here? I'll cook lasagna for her."

"Do you know how to cook lasagna?"

"No, but you do. You could give me your recipe and teach me, but I want to fix it myself."

Somehow I couldn't picture my son, who rarely entered the kitchen except to eat, fixing a gourmet dinner for his date. I decided to voice some other concerns. "How are you paying for all the other expenses?" I asked.

"Sandy's dad said we could use his car. It's a Mercedes. He knows I have a good driving record. We'll get more stares than any of those people in limos. No one else will have a Mercedes."

I nodded to myself, waiting to hear more.

"I saved up some money for the prom ticket, and Sandy's paying for the pictures. It's a piece of cake." A big smile lit up my son's face. He had it all under control. Then his eyes narrowed, and he looked at me sternly. "You did order the flowers, didn't you?" he asked.

I almost laughed. I was concerned about my son getting everything else paid for, and he was worried about my one little responsibility. "Yes, Mike. I'll pick them up Saturday morning and buy all your lasagna ingredients, too. That's the least I can do."

"Thanks, Mom," came his soft reply.

Prom night I sat by the fireplace in the living room, eating a piece of Mike's lasagna, trying not to intrude on the young people. Occasional laughter filtered in from the dining room, and I heard Sandy exclaim, "This is delicious!" They continued their relaxed small talk over their candlelight dinner.

I thought back to my youth and realized what a treat it was for a girl to have her high school beau personally prepare a gourmet meal. I'm sure Sandy felt very special. And I knew this would be a wonderful prom night for my youngest son.

When I had worried about finances, God gave my son the most ingenious ideas to make this special occasion even more memorable. I leaned back on the couch, put my feet up, and completely relaxed. What a special evening this was for all of us.

—*Susan Titus Osborn*

Summer
AND BLUE EYES

"Unlike a baby-sitter, a mother knows she cannot quit and go home at the end of the day. Her love for her child keeps her giving, believing, and teaching at all hours."

—BRENDA HUNTER

"Mom, look! Aren't they adorable? Can we *pleeeease* keep them? You won't have to do anything. I'll take care of 'em, I promise."

Oh no! Thirteen-year-old Jennifer had two kittens in her arms. We didn't have the time or the money for pets. I struggled just getting the laundry done and keeping things organized in our household of eight. She *said*, "I'll take care of them," but I knew these kittens would grow up to be not-so-cute-anymore cats. And guess who would be taking care of them *then*? But looking into Jennifer's wide, expectant eyes, I didn't have the heart to say no.

"Okay, we'll try it, but they have to stay in the garage. No exceptions. And the first time you neglect them, they're history."

"Thanks, Mom. You're the greatest." She gave me a hug and ran off, yelling to her sisters, "Look what I have! Mom said we can keep them!"

Jennifer named her kittens Summer and Blue Eyes, and they were the hit of our family. Amy and Sarah had them attend tea parties and took them on more than one walk in a doll stroller, dressed in baby clothes. They didn't seem to mind, though, and I had to admit Jennifer was following through on her end of our deal.

It wasn't long, however, before we had problems. Three-year-old Amy began wheezing. We discovered that she was severely allergic to cats. Day after day I warned her, "Amy, don't touch those cats. . . . Amy, wash your hands." This was an impossible task for a little girl who loved animals. Her wheezing got worse. The kittens had to go.

We offered them to friends and put signs around the neighborhood, at the supermarket, and in the children's schools. No one would take our kittens. We didn't want to think about the animal shelter, knowing what their fate would be, but it seemed our only option.

I couldn't do it, so my husband took Summer and Blue Eyes on the grim ride to the shelter. He returned more despondent than I'd ever seen him, stating, "Don't ask me to do that again." We all sat down to dinner in total silence.

"Okay, guys, we're going to pray." Immediately all heads bowed. We held tightly to each other's hands, Jennifer brushed tears from her cheek, and I prayed, "Lord, please take care of

Summer and Blue Eyes. They're probably frightened. Find someone who loves blue-eyed kittens and will take good care of them. Amen."

Three days later I opened our local newspaper, and two white, blue-eyed kittens stared back at me from the front page. *Summer and Blue Eyes!* The caption said they had just been brought to the animal shelter and they needed a good home. They were going to be on an adopt-a-pet van at our shopping mall the upcoming weekend.

"Jennifer, Sarah, Amy, look at this!" When they saw the picture, their expressions were priceless. "You know, kids, I've heard good things about this adopt-a-van. Someone is going to fall in love with our kittens and take them home."

Busy moms look for teachable moments. Nothing I could tell my children would ever illustrate more beautifully how God cares for each one of them and all the little details in their lives, including finding homes for two little kittens. He loves us and wants to show us how much. Sometimes He even announces it in the newspaper.

—*Judith Scharfenberg*

Making the decision to have a child is momentous. It is to decide forever to have your heart go walking around outside your body.

—BRENDA HUNTER

28

Journey
TO THE DEPTHS OF MY PURSE

I carry the basic essentials of life in my purse. Aspirin, lipstick, hand lotion, credit cards . . . you name it, it's in there. If it's not, it will be. I seem to have some sort of purse reflex. I can stuff things in there without even knowing it.

On the positive side, I found a five-dollar bill in a sneaky secret pocket last week. Even better, I found a candy bar. Now that was interesting. It was squished—almost liquefied —but it was still inside the wrapper.

Unfortunately, there are other encounters now and then that aren't exactly positive purse experiences. The other day, for example, I was making a return at a local store, and I had to do an emergency receipt search at the customer service counter. Soon my purse stuff started piling up. I pulled out five loose Lifesavers, an old Valentine card, sunscreen, one mitten, six kid-meal toys (including a mini-tractor with only one wheel), three keys of unknown lock origin, and a dead cricket. There were twelve tissues (none I would actually use), last year's Christmas list, a ticket stub to the junior high spring concert, and the backs from four adhesive name tags. But no receipt.

I also found two gummy-worms stuck in a hairbrush, a Denny's coupon that expired in 1997, and a plastic Easter egg. (I was pretty sure that the egg was older than the coupon. I shook it to see if it rattled. It did. I think I made it angry.)

There was also enough purse fuzz in there to stuff a sofa pillow. How embarrassing. Inside the purse fuzz, something green and squishy caught my eye—and it frightened me. I gained courage by tossing the dead cricket and drinking the candy bar.

Just before I dove into the fuzz, I got to the heart of my purse: my mini Bible. It had all my family pictures tucked inside. That's when I realized that everything important in life could be found in my purse.

Okay, if you want to get technical, I didn't exactly find Jesus in my handbag. But I could pull out the pictures of my husband and my children and see reminders of His gifts to me. And His Word was there. Granted, it smelled a little like Juicy Fruit, but it was a great reminder that there's really no place I can go where I won't find the Lord's presence. Not one fuzz-covered place!

I'm rejoicing in His love—even though I never found the receipt.

For the record, I think that green squishy thing used to be a jelly bean. I guess we'll never know. One of the kids ate it.

—*Rhonda Rhea*

This story, originally entitled "Unfinished Business," first appeared in *Home Life* magazine, September 2001. Used by permission.

Part Three
COPING THROUGH TRIALS

Often the storms of life come crashing down on us with the force of an angry sea. Waves of hurt tower over us. Doubts and uncertainty fill our minds. The turbulent waves toss us around like toy ships. Darkness descends upon us, causing apprehension and lack of insight. Learning to cope is hard during those difficult circumstances—especially when God seems so far away. Yet He is there, ready to take our hand and lead us out of the storm.

For our momentary light affliction is producing for us an absolutely incomparable eternal weight of glory. So we do not focus on what is seen, but on what is unseen; for what is seen is temporary, but what is unseen is eternal.

—2 CORINTHIANS 4:17–18

The
BLESSING JAR

Life had been particularly difficult for our family one year. The list of tragic events ran longer than my grocery list. I felt exhausted. Yet my strength was needed to help hold the pieces together.

"Why do I have to take four shots a day?" Jenna Marie, my kindergartner, asked repeatedly. The explanation of being diagnosed with juvenile diabetes didn't seem to satisfy her.

"Just how big is the tank that Uncle Rusty is driving? How far away is the Gulf War? Who is this Saddam guy anyway?" my four-year old son, Jason, questioned.

Beep, beep, beep. . . the steady rhythm of my premature baby Joel's heart monitor was our moment-by-moment reminder of how fragile life really was.

My husband, Marty, and I had learned to expect the unexpected, but lately we had lost our focus. The challenges of life so overwhelmed us that we did not see the blessings that God provided us daily.

As a family, we regularly read of God's faithfulness to Moses, Joseph, and David. "Why can't we read about God's faithfulness to us—the Mitchells?" our children asked.

At a loss for words, I looked to my husband.

After a long moment of silence he said, "We can, and we will! Kids, go get Daddy's special note cards and a box of crayons."

The children hurried off. I sat pondering. I couldn't help but wonder what my non-seminarian husband was thinking.

When the children returned, we all sat Indian-style on the family room floor. Everyone was quiet as Daddy began to speak:

"There are times in our lives when we don't see God's blessings right away. Sometimes they are disguised, and the things we once thought of as bad or scary turn into wonderful blessings. Think of a caterpillar. He isn't very pretty. It has to be a little bit scary for him to seal off the cocoon he's entwined around himself. I wonder if Mr. Caterpillar screams, 'Let me out of here! I can't breathe!' But then one day, just at the right time, we see something happening. We see God's plan, the miracle of a beautiful butterfly.

"Let's think back and remember how God has taken care of us and blessed our family. Then we'll write these blessings on the note cards."

"But Daddy, we can't write words," Jason said.

"We couldn't read them even if we wrote them!" Jenna chimed in.

"You're right," Daddy replied. "But you can draw!"

For the next half hour, our family remembered, drew, laughed, and shed a few tears as we recorded God's faithfulness to the Mitchells.

Later that night I found an old dusty jar. Using leftover puffy-paint, I painted the words "Our Blessing Jar" on the side. I gathered the note cards we had colored and dropped them into the jar. Tying a colorful ribbon around the lid, I left it as the centerpiece on the kitchen table. And sitting next to it, I placed another stack of Daddy's special note cards.

The next morning the children gathered around the table. "What's this?" Jenna asked while opening the lid. "It's our blessings! We have a Blessing Jar! Let's see how many blessings we can think of today!" she shouted with excitement.

"You know, Daddy says that God is the one who gives the blessings. We just need to keep track of them," Jason reported.

And for the past ten years, we have. Our children are now old enough to read for themselves the stories of God's faithfulness to Moses, Joseph, and David. They've learned to trust when they can't see past their cocoons. They know that somehow, some way, a butterfly will emerge. And they know without a doubt who makes the butterfly fly.

Tonight I added another blessing to the Mitchell family's Blessing Jar. "Lord," I wrote, "thanks for the dark nights when challenges knocked on our door like a regular visitor. Thanks for the special note cards and crayons. And thanks for giving us a way to read about Your faithfulness to the Mitchells!"

—*Janet Lynn Mitchell*

Life affords no greater responsibility, no greater privilege than the raising of the next generation.

—C. EVERETT KOOP, M.D.

35

Next to
MY HEART

One of the worst days in my whole life was the day I stopped dead in my tracks in the aisle of a busy supermarket. There I was, pregnant as could be, with charley horses in both feet so excruciating I couldn't move. A whole month past my due date, I was forty pounds overweight. Plus, I had the most awful morning sickness that lasted twenty-four hours every single day.

Motherhood wasn't what I had expected. My own mother, who had raised six children, glowed when she was expecting. My grandmother not only joyfully welcomed sixteen little ones into the world, but also ran a busy store, farm, and home the entire time.

"Looking forward to holding a little one in your arms will cause you to glow," my mother had said over and over. "Feeling the miracle of life inside you will make you ecstatically happy . . . and healthy!" she always added.

In all the magazines I purchased, the maternity advertisements showed blissful mothers-to-be in adorable outfits, perfect hair-dos, and even high-heel shoes. All my expecting friends fit the mold. An officemate with the same due date as mine worked right up until the time her baby came. My next-door neighbor did everything she wanted for nine full months, including lead-ing an active sports and social life. The entire time she looked absolutely gorgeous. Neither friend had been ill for a minute, and both of them now had adorable, healthy babies.

Meanwhile, I was still pregnant, still miserable, and so large I had long since forgotten what either my feet or my legs looked like. There was only one outfit I could get into—a sort of muumuu tent. I'd given up working, given up church ministries, and almost given up hope.

Why was God allowing this to happen to me? He knew I loved Him, my husband, and this unborn child. My friends had started snickering, "You were due *when?*" Even my doctor grumped at me as if it were completely my fault.

And now during one of the hottest Augusts on record, my ankles swelled so badly in our sweltering apartment, I had to keep them in buckets of ice most of the time. Going anywhere was torture, but we were out of milk. *Just a quick dash to the store,* I thought. *Surely I can do that.*

So here I stood, frozen in my tracks, stopping carts in both directions. My face beet red, I stared at the rows of cracker boxes in front of me, pretending not to notice the angry shoppers whose way I was blocking.

Then I heard a little girl's voice, "Mommy, why does that lady look so funny?"

I squeezed my eyes shut, trying to stop sudden tears, as I said a silent prayer. *Oh, God, please! That's the last straw! Can't anyone say anything nice about me for a change? I'm so tired of being a medical freak. Won't I ever look normal and feel comfortable again? Won't I ever get to hold this baby in my arms?*

Then that mother said something I will never forget: "She looks that way, dear, because God has given her a tiny baby to carry next to her heart."

When I opened my eyes, mother and daughter were gone.

Eventually, so were the charley horses. But those words have stayed with me for a lifetime.

For, oh, they were so true—and such a blessing to me during those final miserable days before I did hold my beautiful first-born child in my arms. During my next two pregnancies, I often thought of those very same words. They were a blessing I remembered as my three children grew up and married. Then they became a blessing I have been privileged to share with my own pregnant daughters-in-law and many other young women I have known over the years.

For even after our children are born, all of us mothers still carry those precious little ones next to our hearts—even when they are grown and have children of their own. And they remain next to our hearts our whole lives long.

—*Bonnie Compton Hanson*

The best and most beautiful things in the world cannot be seen or touched . . . but are felt in the heart.

—HELEN KELLER

Tommy's TRIUMPH

Five-year-old Tommy stood at the front of the chapel, his fingers wrapped comfortably around a microphone. "Genesis, Exodus, Leviticus . . ."

The small congregation watched as the boy continued without the slightest hesitation. "Ezra, Nehemiah, Esther . . ."

Unaware of the building tension in the room, Tommy spoke as calmly as if he were listing his favorite cartoon characters. "Ezekiel, Daniel, Hosea . . ." Could this child really recite the names of all sixty-six books of the Bible—in their proper order?

Parishioners leaned forward in their pews. A few of them stole glances at the table of contents in the Bibles on their laps.

Dressed in a plaid vest, clip-on bow tie, dress slacks, and scuffed-up tennis shoes, Tommy stood tall, his brown hair meticulously combed off to one side. His voice never wavered as he spoke with the confidence of a seasoned preacher. "Zechariah, Malachi . . ."

I sat on the edge of my seat in the front pew, eyes riveted to Tommy's face, my hands clasped tightly. I had spent countless hours memorizing with my son. Every day after work, Tommy had begged me to help him with his special project. I was happy to oblige. I knew each moment with him was a precious gift from God.

You see, I had conceived Tommy when I was an unwed teenager. My original plan was to place my baby for adoption. But as the baby grew inside me, I became convinced that—with God's help—I could raise this child myself.

Children are an invaluable gift from God, a treasure of which we must be careful stewards.

—CHARLES STANLEY

I encountered numerous struggles as a single mom. What pained me most was leaving my little boy in day care while I worked full-time. But Tommy never complained. Every morning, he wrapped chubby arms around my neck and gave me a tight hug before trotting off to join his friends. When I returned, he raced into my arms and planted a sloppy kiss on my cheek. His "I love you, Mommy" made all my struggles melt into insignificance.

After some searching I found a church whose congregation accepted me and my son without judgment. Tommy came home from Sunday school, singing about the "B-I-B-L-E." When he asked me to help him memorize the books of the Bible, it seemed an overwhelming task. I didn't know all the names myself! I wasn't even sure how to pronounce some of them. And when would I find the time? But I agreed to try.

It hadn't been easy. But whenever he became discouraged,

Tommy folded his hands, bowed his head, squeezed his eyes shut, and asked for God's help. As I prayed with him, I thanked the Lord for the amazing treasure He had allowed me to hold.

So there I sat on the edge of that front pew, making a conscious effort to release my lower lip from between my teeth as Tommy's recital flowed effortlessly. "Galatians, Ephesians, Philippians . . . "

Shuffling feet stilled. Even breathing seemed to cease throughout the chapel as Tommy glided flawlessly through the home stretch. "First, Second, and Third John, Jude, Revelation."

Gasps mixed with sighs as the congregation finally breathed. Then thunderous applause shook the stained-glass windows.

Pastor Jensen accepted the microphone from Tommy and took a deep breath before he spoke. "When I promised a brand-new Bible to anyone who could list all the books of the Old and New Testaments," he announced, his words barely escaping past the constriction in his throat, "I never expected it to be presented to a five-year-old boy." He knelt and placed a thick, leather Bible into Tommy's outstretched arms.

I leapt from my seat, rushed up to my son, and wrapped him in a smothering embrace. "I'm so proud of you," I whispered. The cheers of the congregation nearly drowned out my words.

"I'm proud of you, too," he declared, looking up at me with unabashed admiration.

As I led Tommy back to the front pew, his "I love you, Mommy" made all my struggles melt into insignificance once again.

—*Kathy Ide*

Part Four

GETTING AWAY FROM IT ALL

When we become stressed out and the tension starts to build, we need to find a place where we can get away. We need rest to rejuvenate our bodies, our minds, and our souls. A vacation can be a few days at the beach or the mountains, or it can entail a flight to an exotic location. Or we can take a ten-minute vacation by just leaning back in our favorite chair and closing our eyes. If we can escape temporarily from our busy schedules, perhaps we can find time to spend in solitude with God.

But when you pray, go into your private room, shut your door, and pray to your Father who is in secret. And your Father who sees in secret will reward you.

—MATTHEW 6:6

The
INVITATION

"Could you take Carl and me to the beach today, Mom?" asked my fifteen-year-old son, Mike. "Carl's mom is working. She can't do it."

I glanced at my desk, piled high with papers from my latest writing assignment. Then I eyed a stack of unpaid bills shoved on the counter. "I don't think so, Mike. I've got to stay on target for my book deadline. Plus, I've got to pay bills today."

"Oh, Mom. There's a tropical storm in the Pacific. The waves are supposed to be fantastic!" Mike looked at me, his big blue eyes pleading. When I didn't reply, he continued, "It would give me a chance to try out the new surfboard you gave me for my birthday. Pretty please?"

I looked at my son's expression and realized how important this was to him. Then I looked once again at my desk. I could take some of my notes with me and try to organize my thoughts while we were at the beach. Then at least the whole day wouldn't be wasted. The bills could wait until tomorrow.

"Okay, go call Carl and tell him we'll pick him up in an hour," I said.

"Thanks, Mom, you're the greatest!" Mike gave me a quick hug and raced to the phone to call his best friend.

I went into the kitchen and started packing a picnic lunch.

Soon Mike and Carl were loading surfboards onto the rack on top of my station wagon and we were off.

Several hours later I sat in my sand chair and dug my toes into the cool, moist sand. I breathed deeply the fresh, salty air and felt my body totally relax. What a gift from God this set-ting was.

I looked out at the line of surfers sitting on their boards and waiting for the perfect wave. Mike was easy to spot because his new board was glow-in-the-dark orange. Soon a huge wave started rolling, and Mike stood up and rode it into shore.

He ran over to me laughing, his new board tucked under his arm. "Did you see me, Mom? That wave was perfect!"

"Yes, I did. Your surfing has really improved since the last time I watched you," I said.

Mike gave me a look that needed no words. I was proud of my son and his athletic ability, and he knew it. Plus, he realized that I was willing to give up *my* time to spend quality time with *him.* That meant so much to him.

The following year he would be sixteen, and I might not receive any more invitations to go to the beach. He would be able to drive himself, so he wouldn't need me.

Life isn't a matter of milestones, but of moments.

—ROSE KENNEDY

Another big wave crested, and I watched the owner of the bright orange surfboard ride it smoothly to shore. *I would have missed these moments if I hadn't come today.* I thanked the Lord for touching my heart and allowing me this special time with my youngest son.

—*Susan Titus Osborn*

The Road
WORRIER

*Look for the light of God that is
hitting your life, and you will find
sprinkles you didn't know were there.*

—BARBARA JOHNSON

"Vacation." Just mention the word, and you can expect some multifaceted responses. Some vacationer-wannabes immediately envision enjoying a tropical breeze, basking on a beach. For other vacationers—especially those with children—it can cause flashbacks of a toddler throwing up on the map, cross-country potty stops, red slushy upholstery stains, and shooting leers toward the backseat that could stop bullets. Me? I would have to go with a little of both.

Most of the time, I get to choose. Will I have a warm, fuzzy, beach-type moment, or will I end up banging my head repeatedly against the dashboard? It has a lot to do with my own attitude, my vacation expectations, and my contentment level. I can choose to fuss and fret my trip away. That's when I become . . . "The Road Worrier."

By the way, I'm writing this juicy little morsel while vacationing. At this moment we're semi-fuzzy. But, as you might imagine, with five kids and two adults packed into a minivan (along with enough luggage to clothe a third-world nation), the trip has not been without flashback-inducing moments. At the last several rest room stops, I pressed my face against my passenger side window and, just for fun, slowly mouthed the words, "Help me!" to anyone who would look.

I think the authorities are looking for me in four states.

Since I'm a Texas-grown gal, I'm happy to say that Texas is one of those four. Vacations are bigger in Texas. They grow everything bigger in Texas. Sadly, that also includes the bugs. I'm scratching even now. Even though we slathered ourselves with drums of cancer-causing repellent, I was pretty sure we'd be toast against these Texas bugs. Sure enough, I was right. We've been *Texas* Toast. It's like running into a herd of Bugzillas. I think there are more varieties of bugs in Texas than there are in the rain forest. They all bite. This might interest an entomologist, but I'm not an entomologist.

As a matter of fact, as I was reaching for my notepad to start this story, I came close to causing a major pile-up on I-30. I opened my notepad and saw bug legs. I just about scared my husband right off the highway and on into Arkansas. But don't worry—a little CPR and he'll be just fine.

The bug, however, is dead. He was already deceased when I opened my notebook. But unfortunately for my husband, dead bug legs look exactly like live bug legs. I stopped screaming as soon as I realized the legs weren't attached to a bug body. You may want to send those cards to my husband at home, where he's recovering nicely, thank you.

There are choices along every journey: Warm, fuzzy thoughts or head-banging. Contentment or crabbiness. Resting or worrying. Learning to rest is learning to trust. And we have the same choices all along our everyday Christian journey. We can rest in the Lord and make an effort to invoke more warm fuzzies, or we can crab and worry about every bump in the road.

Trying to find contentment anywhere other than Christ won't work in any state—even Texas. Don't try it. That would be goofier than screaming at dead bug legs.

One more word of vacation advice: Make sure you put the trail mix in zip-lock bags instead of those fold-over things. If you ignore this warning and put it in the fold-overs anyway, then at least make sure you check the raisins before you start snacking. If they have legs, don't eat them.

For the record, the leg test is not a foolproof one. Sometimes the legs are not attached.

—*Rhonda Rhea*

This story was first published in *Home Life* magazine, June 2001. Used by permission.

Savoring
SIMPLE PLEASURES

Remember this old Shaker tune?

'Tis a gift to be simple, 'tis a gift to be free,
'Tis a gift to come down where you ought to be.

I had an opportunity once to experience the wisdom of this gentle message when I needed it most. My husband, Charles, and I had slipped away for a weekend alone at our cozy cabin in the mountains. Late Saturday afternoon after a long day spent raking pine needles and pulling weeds in the yard, I hobbled into the house—exhausted. Everything about me ached. All I wanted was a warm tub and a bowl of hot soup!

Charles stayed behind to put away the gardening tools. I settled into the soapy water, took a deep breath, and relaxed for the first time that day. What a blessing! We were alone. No teenagers hanging on the phone, asking for the next meal, or begging to stay out past eleven.

But still my mind wouldn't settle down! Thoughts raced ahead as I considered all the things left to do before our little house was just the way I wanted it. Wallpaper for the bathroom. Rugs for the living room and bedroom. Pretty curtains for the windows. And of course, it would be nice to buy a new sofa-bed and a matching chair and some kitchen dishes and put up family photos on the walls and . . . wouldn't it be fun to start a small garden out back? And . . .

A hard rap on the bathroom window pulled me out of my fantasy. I ran my hand over the steamy window pane and looked out. There stood Charles smiling at me, his face

50

*This is what I want from now on:
a slower pace, a more centered existence,
and the feelings of perfect happiness
to be found in the moments I come
home to myself.*

—LINDA WELTNER

smudged, his eyes bright. He pulled off his cap and wiped the beads of perspiration that poured down his face.

What's up?" I called.

"Not much," he answered. "I miss you, that's all. The sun's almost down," he added gently, pointing toward the mountains, "and I want you here beside me as the day ends."

A little shiver ran down my spine. Here was a gesture so simple, a gift so lovely, it took my breath away. It also brought me down to where I ought to be. I suddenly had a fresh vision of Jesus—in my husband's words and in his face.

I realized I was being a Martha when it was clearly time to be a Mary. What did it matter in that moment that we didn't have everything in place? We had each other. We had our children. We had the Lord. We had this day.

I suddenly realized what a gift it is to be simple—to be free— and to make time for a rest stop.

I grabbed a towel, slipped into my bathrobe, and dashed out back—just in time to enjoy the simple pleasure of watching, arm-in-arm with my husband, the golden sun slip behind the hills.

—*Karen O'Connor*

Part Five
RECOGNIZING ANGELS

A special word of hope can reach us in many ways. It may come from a friend or family member who is close to us, or it may come from a total stranger. Can these people who walk briefly into our lives be angels sent from God? Their words spoken at just the right time lift our spirits and help us to soar on the wings of eagles. These special angels bring us just the encouragement we need to help us continue our journey through life.

For He will give His angels orders concerning you, to protect you in all your ways. They will support you with their hands so that you will not strike your foot against a stone.

—PSALM 91:11–12

Malinda,
MY SPECIAL ANGEL

"Hey, I didn't see you come in," Malinda greeted me with a hug.

Turning to gather up the scattered papers from around my chair, I explained, "I was running late from work, so I just sat in the back. It seemed like it was a great Bible study today, though."

As we stood and faced each other, she reached out and grabbed my hand. "Are you getting excited about Philip coming to live with you and Al next week?" she asked.

I smiled weakly, while my eyes filled up with tears. "Yes, but I am just so . . ."

As I choked on my words, Malinda hugged me tightly. "What is it, sweetie? What are you worried about?" she asked tenderly. "You'll be a great mom."

"But I have never been one before," I sobbed. "And Philip needs so much right now with his mother dying and everything else that has happened in his life."

Malinda grabbed both my hands and looked into my eyes. "You'll be just what he needs. I know you will," she assured me.

"I don't know, Malinda. I am terrified. I have a full-time job. I've never raised a child, and he's a teenager!" I said as I wiped the tears off my face.

"You're going to be a great mom. God will be there with you every step of the way." Malinda gave me a big, warm smile and a reassuring hug. Then we each climbed into our separate cars.

As I drove home I thought about what she had said. I knew she was right about God's part, but I wasn't so sure about mine.

I reached my street with tears streaming down my face, and I began to pray: "Dear Lord, thank you for this wonderful child you are giving me. I know your hand is in all of this, but I just hope I'm the right woman for the job."

Slowly, out of habit, I stopped beside the mailbox to get the mail. As I mindlessly thumbed through the bills and advertisements, I saw a light blue envelope addressed to me. As I read the enclosed note, I couldn't believe my eyes.

"Dear Child of God, I'm an angel sent from above to guide you and direct you in your new adventure as a mom. When you want an extra dose of love, I'll have plenty to share. When you need a helping of patience, I will provide. When you desire a cup full of wisdom, I'll pour it with generosity, and when you ache for rest, I'll be your comfort. I can give you all of this because in God's love there is no lack. With love . . . Your Special Angel."

Once again I was overtaken with tears, but these were tears of joy. God had spoken to someone about my pain even before I knew how I felt. And best of all, these words had arrived exactly when I needed them most.

I flipped the blue envelope back over to look at the postmark, where it read: Magnolia, Texas. "Malinda! It's from Malinda!" I exclaimed to myself. "My angel, my friend, and God's timely messenger."

God had been speaking to me all along, if only I had stopped to listen. "A great mom," I pondered out loud. "A great mom!" I said again with enthusiasm.

As I put the car in park, I glanced in the rearview mirror and sure enough, there she was—Philip's new mom!

—*Rebecca Dowden*

A friend is an angel, always watching over you.

—GAIL GOODWIN

My four-year-old son had been waking up nearly every night for six months having nightmares. "The Grinch is going to get me," Chase exclaimed through tears as he clung to me in the dark.

I tried to explain that the Grinch wasn't real. I told him, "Monsters and grinches are just made up, but God sends angels to watch over you all of the time. And angels are real." This seemed to make him feel better, and eventually he'd fall back asleep.

One day he came to me and asked, "What are angels?"

I explained, "They are special beings that God sends to watch over us and keep us safe, but you can't see them." As days passed I began to think more about angels and how I could explain them to Chase in a way he could understand. But I soon realized that God was sending us "angels" all the time that we actually *could* see. We just didn't recognize them because we were so busy running to preschool or dashing home for nap-time. So I started to pay attention.

Soon I began to notice the man who let me go ahead of him in the grocery line when I had two fussy little boys trying to climb out of the cart. I thought about moms at the park who offered a friendly ear around the sandbox when I hadn't had any adult conversation all day. I was very sick during one pregnancy, and friends brought dinners to my husband, Ken, so that I wouldn't have to cook. I came to realize that I had gifts from God surrounding me everyday, and I hadn't even noticed.

I tried to explain to Chase what I had learned. I said, "Not only does God send heavenly angels to watch over us, but also He wants to demonstrate His love for us by putting people in our lives everyday to help us when we need them. God uses people to be sort of like angels to us."

He thought about this for a minute. "You mean like when someone pushes me on the playground and a friend helps me up?"

"Yes," I replied.

"Or like when the man at the ice cream place gives me extra ice cream?"

"Well, I guess so," I said.

He smiled, satisfied. "Boy, God must love us a lot to think of all those things."

"Chase, He loves you even more than you can imagine. We get so caught up in our own lives that we forget. He sends those kind of 'angels' to help us remember."

Chase thought for a moment. "I guess if God loves me that much, I don't have to worry about monsters or grinches or anything anymore."

"That's right," I replied.

"I like angels, Mommy."

"So do I, Chase."

Now I try and make it a point not to miss even one blessing God sends to me or my family. I remember the friends who were there to hold my hand as I watched the events of September 11 unfold on a television at church, afraid to leave my children alone at preschool. There was a brief time when—

due to some tough circumstances—we didn't have health insurance, and the nurses at the pediatrician's office came up with the exact amount of sample antibiotics my kids needed that would have cost us hundreds of dollars.

Chase was right: If God loves us enough to think of all of those things, we don't need to be afraid of monsters or grinches or anything.

—*Cindy Barber*

The most important things in your home are people.

—BARBARA JOHNSON

We Met
AN ANGEL TODAY

I have held many things in my hand,

and I have lost them all,

but whatever I have

placed in God's hands,

that I still possess.

—AUTHOR UNKNOWN

Most of our friends said, "Don't do it."

In fact, I can remember my mom's advice as I grew up: "Don't ever have kids." It was more than the usual concerns. Genetic counseling indicated we had a 50 percent chance that our offspring would be born without legs, just like me. The thought of myself, a disabled woman, mothering a disabled child seemed an overwhelming proposition. Subsequent counseling gave us more hope, however, suggesting that our offspring had merely a five-hundredths of a percent chance (the normal risk) of inheriting my birth defect.

My husband, David, and I waited ten years before starting our family. Once we did, our first child nearly arrived before we could leave the house. But thanks to the paramedics, I was whisked into the emergency room ten minutes before delivery. David counted two healthy legs—with perfectly formed feet and ten toes—before rejoicing that our baby was a little girl. We named her Emily.

Mothering Emily was a daily adventure. With trial and error I learned which jobs worked best in my wheelchair and which ones worked better when I wore my artificial limbs.

Emily adapted to me intuitively, tucking her chin into my shoulder to steady herself when I walked. She grew to be Mama's helper. She picked up things I dropped and retrieved what I needed from the other room, eager to share the strength of her two legs.

The day I realized that Emily and I could manage mothering was the day I wanted more children. Next came Elizabeth. And even after she was born I longed for one more, and soon baby number three was on the way.

Then one day I was sure I'd bitten off more than I could chew. Eight months pregnant with our third child, I was running late for my 10:30 doctor's appointment. Wearily, I loaded my wheelchair into our adapted van, strapped the two girls into their car seats, and hoisted myself into the driver's seat. I felt like a mother elephant.

Disappointed to see the handicapped parking spaces occupied at the hospital entrance, I parked down the hill. Turning off the ignition, I sat in a daze, doubting my strength to make it to the top of this morning's mountain.

That's when I noticed him—a middle-aged man standing in front of my van. Our eyes met. He smiled and walked to my door. I rolled down the window and heard his welcome words, "What can I do to help?"

Too fatigued to ask him how he knew I needed help, I talked him through the unloading ritual. First, he got out my wheelchair. Next he helped me into it. He carefully lifted two-year-old Elizabeth onto my lap and situated four-year-old Emily at my side. I rested as he pushed my chair up the incline and through the automatic doors around the corner to the elevator. After he pressed the elevator button, I turned to thank him, but no one was there.

I proceeded to my doctor's appointment, then to the grocery store. The girls and I had lunch and took naps. I cooked and served dinner, cleaned up the kitchen, and put Elizabeth to bed.

When all was done, Emily and I snuggled side-by-side in our favorite rocker. Reviewing our day, I thought of the man who had come to our rescue. "How could he have known of our need?" I asked more to myself than to Emily.

Suddenly it hit me—a realization gently germinating all day! I remembered God's promise of angels sent to help and care for us . . . unawares. I was filled with awe as I looked down at my daughter. "Emily, I think we might have met an angel today."

—*Judith Ann Squier*

Part Six

SPECIAL MOMENTS TO REMEMBER

As we look back over our lives, some of the most memorable moments are special occasions such as birthdays and weddings. They may also be times when we or someone close to us received a special award or honor. Other moments which turn out to be just as memorable may seem at the time to be commonplace and insignificant. Yet life is made up of these tiny moments, and we should treasure them in our hearts.

I will thank the Lord with all my heart; I will declare all Your wonderful works. I will rejoice and boast about You; I will sing about Your name, Most High.

—PSALM 9:1-2

The Apron
STRINGS

One of the most difficult times for me as a mother was allowing my oldest son to go away to college. When he graduated from high school, I wrote him the following letter:

"Dear Richard,

"Today is your high school graduation. I have spent the last eighteen years teaching and guiding you. Now it is time to let you go and allow you to choose your own way.

"As you were growing up, I shared your victories and defeats. I cheered at your swim meets and applauded at your cello concerts. I watched a skinny, freckle-faced, blonde boy change into a handsome, six-foot-three, muscular young man.

"As a mother, the hardest job for me is to let go—to allow our roles to change. I worked hard at being your mother, and now I want to enjoy being your friend. As a token of my feelings and my confidence in you, I'm enclosing my apron strings in this letter. They are cut off from my apron to symbolize your total freedom.

"Yet you know that I will be only a phone call away. I want to continue to share your life, to hear about your experiences, to be there when you need me. The difference is that now you are in the driver's seat and I'm the passenger.

"I believe in you, and I love you very much.
Congratulations, Son!

"All my love . . . Mom"

We spend many years as busy moms helping our children develop strong roots. As they grow older we hope they will continue to build on that foundation. Yet the time comes to cut the apron strings and permit them to fly away. By doing this we allow them to lead their own lives, make their own decisions, and accept the responsibility for their own mistakes.

At the time of Richard's graduation, problems in my own life made it especially difficult for me to cut the apron strings. My husband and I had talked about obtaining a legal separation, and eventually we divorced. Because of my loneliness, I found myself clinging to my children even though I realized it was wrong. With prayerful help from God, I was able to release Richard to Him and still maintain a close family atmosphere without smothering my grown son.

I often look back to the day seventeen years ago when I wrote that letter to a high school graduate.

I compare that with the relationship I now have with my thirty-five-year-old son. He is truly one of my best friends. Although his present job takes him around the world, he continues to keep in touch by telephone and email.

No matter how many miles separate me from my firstborn, we will always be close. When he is in town, we work at making time in our busy schedules for each other. Over dinner I share his adventures and his dreams as I always have, and I hope I always will.

—Susan Titus Osborn

This story is adapted from a story in *Rest Stops for Single Moms*, authored by Susan Titus Osborn and Lucille Moses, published by Broadman & Holman Publishers, 1995, 2000. Used with permission.

*There are only two lasting things
we can give our children.
One is roots; the other, wings.*

—AUTHOR UNKNOWN

Jimmy's BIKE

"Oh, help! What am I going to do now?" My husband's six-year-old son, Jimmy, had just come to live with us. I had no idea what to do with a little boy. I'd never been around kids at all, and I had a full-time job to keep me busy.

A few days after he arrived, he asked, "Can I play outside?"

Praying for wisdom, I said, "Okay, but be careful."

I found out later that he'd gone up the hill, knocking on every door and asking, "Do you have any little boys for me to play with?" To his delight, he found a house at the top of the hill with not one, but two little boys. The boys had a great time playing together.

At the beginning of summer, both his friends received bicycles. My husband, Roy, promised Jimmy that we would get him a bike, too. However, Roy left town the next day on business.

The day after he left, Jimmy kept asking, "Are we going to get my bike now, Mom? Can we go now?" I stalled and stalled, hoping he would wait until his father got home, but finally I said, "Let's go look for a bike."

Off we went to Sears, where we looked at every single bike. Finally he settled on a nice red one. But when they brought out our purchase—to my horror—it was unassembled! I prayed, "Oh, help, Lord! What am I going to do?"

Once we got the bike home, Jimmy said, "I want to ride my bike *now*, Mom!"

"Oh, Jimmy! I bought you the bike like you wanted. Can't you wait until tomorrow for Daddy to put it together?"

"No, Mom. I want to ride it now! You can put it together, I know you can!"

He had more faith in me than I did. What did I know about assembling a bicycle? We ripped into the carton. "Careful, Jimmy! We don't want to lose any of the pieces!"

"Oh, boy! Oh, boy!" Jimmy danced around the family room. "My own bike! My own bike! Hurry up, Mom!"

With great dread I read the directions and set off to find the tools I needed to put it together. Fortunately (or perhaps unfortunately) the tools were right where they belonged. "I guess there's no putting this off!" I groused to myself.

Following the directions, I laid out the pieces and began to figure out how to connect them. Jimmy could hardly contain his excitement. Finally, after a couple of incorrect attempts and what seemed like hours, the completely assembled bike stood before us. I tightened a couple of the bolts, not really sure it would hold up when Jimmy tried to ride it. Then we wheeled it outside through the garage where

Jimmy mounted and rode it around the parking area.

"It works! It works! I knew you could do it! My very own bike!" Jimmy was in ecstasy. "I'm going to go show it to my friends," he said, pushing it up the hill.

When Roy got home the next evening, all he had to do was tighten a couple of bolts. How about that? I had put it together correctly. Imagine my surprise when a couple of days later, Jimmy's friends' mom related to me that Jimmy was riding around the neighborhood bragging about his bike. "My bike's special. Mom built my bike!"

"Didn't you know that for an extra ten bucks, Sears would have assembled it for you?" she asked, laughing.

"They would have?" I could have saved myself all that agony, but how was I to know?

As I thought about it later, I mused that maybe this was the way it was meant to be. I'd received a big lesson in the faith of a little child. All things are possible with prayer and some encouragement!

—*Deb Haggerty*

Kind words can be short and easy to speak, but their echoes are truly endless.

—MOTHER TERESA

The Egg
EPISODE

"Mama!" My daughter, then four, called to me from her bedroom. Quickly, I placed four eggs in a pot of water, turned the burner on high and headed down the hall.

Anna sat propped up on a pile of pillows in her room, looking sleepy. Yellow sun stretched across the bed in long narrow strips. It was naptime.

Thou that hast given so much to me,
give one thing more—
a grateful heart.

—GEORGE HERBERT

"What's up?" I asked her.

"Will you read me a story?"

"Okay, but just one. Mommy's boiling eggs."

She nodded. Together we nestled down between the cool sheets and shared the travails of Timothy Tiger and his terrible toothache. Halfway through the book, Anna's eyes drooped. She yawned, slipping further down into the covers. In minutes, she was napping peacefully.

I lay the book aside and curled up next to her, eggs forgotten.

About an hour later, I was awakened by a putrid smell. In the kitchen, sitting atop a bright red burner, an empty, dry pot smoked profusely. To my horror, the eggs had exploded!

Everywhere I looked, pieces of sooty egg lay scattered about. There was egg on the floor, egg on the cabinets, egg on the ceiling, and egg on the countertops. There was even egg in the adjacent room! What an awful, disgusting mess.

Muttering, I reached for a broom and began swiping at the splotches on the ceiling. Then I crawled onto the counter to get a better aim. While I was working and moaning, Anna strolled in, holding her nose.

"Yuck! Whasat I smell?" she asked. Upon seeing me perched high above her, she gasped, "Mama, what on earf happened?"

With little enthusiasm, I related the entire story, ending with, "Look at this mess! I am just sick!" My voice rose with hysteria.

Her answer shocked me. "Well, you oughta be happy," she scolded, her little face solemn.

I glared down at her, speechless. *Happy? Did she say happy?*

"It coulda burned our house down, couldn't it, Mama?" she asked, her brown eyes piercing mine like chocolate daggers. "And it coulda burned us up, too! Couldn't it, Mama? And that would make Daddy so sad. Wouldn't it, Mama?"

Climbing down from the counter, I set my broom aside and stooped down to where my little daughter stood, wondering how on earth I ever got along without such unfathomable wisdom. Cupping her little, round face in my hands, I watched Anna's expression soften. "You are so right, my sweet angel," I said, feeling foolish. "You are one hundred percent right. I should be happy."

Backing up a step, she put her hands on her hips. "And you oughta tell God you're sorry for being so upset." Her little face was suddenly stern again.

Quickly, I did as I was told. For this child of mine had just made me realize how blessed I am—even with eggs plastered all over the kitchen.

—*Dayle Allen Shockley*

Adapted from the book *Whispers from Heaven* by Dayle Allen Shockley, published by Pacific Press. Used with permission.

Part Seven
LOVE THROUGH ACTIONS

It is easy to say the words, "I love you," but it is much harder to show love through the things we do. Our actions speak much louder than our words. The recipient of a loving act will long remember that moment when someone gave of his or her time or went the extra mile to help. Similar examples are visible to us in the legacy that Christ portrayed when He was here on earth. Thus, through the Christlike examples of others, we are able to grasp a glimpse of God. And perhaps they, too, can see Him in the special things we do.

Be alert, stand firm in the faith, be brave and strong. Your every action must be done with love.

—1 CORINTHIANS 16:13–14

The
CONSERVATORY

"Mom, guess what?" my son, Richard, huffed as he raced in the front door after school one day. "I've been invited to play in a special orchestra. It's at a conservatory down by the beach."

'That's quite an honor, Richard," I said as I dried my hands on a towel. Although it was late afternoon, I was just getting around to the morning dishes. Daily I juggled going to college part-time and doing community and church volunteer work with my career as a freelance writer. Plus, I had to sandwich in being a full-time wife, housekeeper, and chauffeur for my twelve- and fourteen-year-old boys.

Sitting down to catch his breath, Richard continued. "Some people from the conservatory came to school today, Mom. We had tryouts during orchestra. It was so cool! We all played two pieces for them, and they chose me!"

"I'm proud of you, Richard. All those hours of practicing your cello are now paying off." I walked over and gave my oldest son a big hug. "When do you start rehearsals?"

"Well, Mom, it's one of the top orchestras in Orange County. We'll practice on Tuesday and Thursday evenings from 7:00-9:00 p.m. down at the conservatory. They don't let parents come to the rehearsals, but you and Dad can come to all the concerts." Richard rambled on and on, telling me every detail he could remember.

Meanwhile, I was thinking of the logistics of fitting another activity into my own busy schedule. I knew I couldn't let Richard miss this exciting opportunity. I thought we could set up carpools with the other kids who made the orchestra. That would help a lot.

"Who else was chosen from your school?" I asked.

"Nobody, Mom," he replied. "I was the only one." He smiled with satisfaction.

"No one," I repeated softly. Suddenly it dawned on me that I would have to drive him to the conservatory twice a week. The beach was about forty-five minutes away from our house, so I wouldn't have time to come home in between. And since parents weren't allowed to listen, I'd have to find someplace to hang out in a strange neighborhood for two hours every Tuesday and Thursday night!

I felt overwhelmed, but I tried not to let it show in my expression. How could I spare two nights away from my latest book project? I was already on a tight schedule, working part-time and taking nine units at the local university. Only the evenings were left for me to write my book.

I paused for a moment, staring off into space, trying to collect my thoughts. But when I looked up at my son's expectant face,

I couldn't say no. God would work it out. I would have to trust Him.

"Well, won't this be a fun outing for just the two of us then? When do we begin?" I asked.

"It starts in two weeks, Mom, and runs for the whole semester. I knew you'd come through for me. You always do."

God does work in mysterious ways. That whole semester, I drove Richard to the conservatory to practice twice a week. And wouldn't you know it, I found a coffee shop nearby that was open until midnight.

Actually, spending two nights a week in a quiet coffee shop was wonderful. There was no one to talk to and no interruptions. I gained four hours of quality writing time each week and three hours of quality time with my son as we drove down there and back. And Richard's cello playing improved tremendously. What a blessing the whole experience turned out to be.

—*Susan Titus Osborn*

When you say yes, say it quickly. But always take a half hour to say no, so you can understand the other fellow's side. —FRANCES CARDINAL SPELLMAN

Anna's
GIFT

It was only 10:00 A.M., and already my day was a complete disaster.

Maybe it was my toddler's constant need for attention or the fact that he was on his third temper tantrum of the day. Maybe it was the endless pile of laundry on the sofa or the fact that I couldn't see my kitchen countertop through all the dirty dishes. Or maybe it was that I had been working in my home office through most of the night and only had a few hours of sleep. There's no telling what caused my breakdown, but something pushed me over the edge.

With my sweet little Nick watching in curious horror, I collapsed into a heap of tears on the living room floor. It was one of the lowest moments of my life. Right then and there I actually prayed out loud, "Lord, I can't live through this day on my own! Please, God! I just can't do this anymore!"

I begged God for supernatural intervention—in a way I never had before. My physical and emotional energy was spent, and yet there was still so much to be done that day. How desperately I wanted help, but I didn't know whom to ask—or even how!

Then within moments the phone rang.

"What's up?" a sweet, unsuspecting voice asked.

It was Anna, a friend from church whom I'd only known a little while. What would she think if I told her how over-whelmed and burdened I felt? Strangely compelled to maintain my façade of perfection, I decided not to tell her the truth. "We're just, uh, hanging out," I said.

"Well," she was cheery, almost excited, "I was just calling to see if I could steal your son for the rest of the day."

Astonished, it was all I could do not to fall back to the floor. Anna was a busy mother herself! She had two small children and worked long shifts as a nurse three days a week. She probably needed a break even more than I did! And yet she was making this incredible and selfless proposal. I swallowed my pride, stifled the urge to protest, and accepted her generous offer.

With Nick gone for the day, I'd be able to get the chores done quickly, have time for a much-needed nap, and perhaps even get more work done in the office before dinner. It was unbelievable!

Just minutes later, I approached Anna's car outside to hand him over. "I've been having a horrible day, Anna," I confessed sheepishly as she rolled down her window to greet me. "Right before you called I was actually crying on my knees, begging God to intervene. You don't know how grateful I am that you're taking Nick for me. You're such an answer to prayer!"

A kind and compassionate act is often its own reward.

—WILLIAM JOHN BENNETT

Anna's eyes widened in surprise, and then she started to cry. "You know what? I had a really bad day at work myself yesterday," she explained over the clamor of our children's happy voices. "And I woke up this morning with this overwhelming need to do something nice for a friend, thinking somehow it would make me feel better," she smiled through the tears. "And it has! I'm so glad I can do this for you!"

We embraced before she left—bonded by our mutual struggles and the blessings we had both discovered through her kindness. God used her in a way that was, for me, unforgettable. Soon we began helping each other with children and chores on a regular basis. Without being asked. Without strings attached.

Perhaps that day was not such a disaster after all.

—*Tamara Rice*

Play
SHOES

A little work, a little play,
to keep us going—and so, good day!

—GEORGE LOUIS PALMELLA BUSSON DU MAURIER

I had my arms full of folded laundry as I scurried from room to room, my three-year-old son, Josiah, tagging along behind me. He had never taken long naps, and now he had given them up altogether. I'm afraid I needed his nap more than he did.

"Mommy, let's play!" he said as I stuffed clean socks into the top drawer of his dresser.

I slammed the drawer shut, yanked open another, and shoved his T-shirts into it. Inwardly I seethed at all the people who had advised me, "Play with your children. Your housework will still be there long after they're gone." *Where,* I wondered, *do such people store eighteen years of dirty laundry?*

I also questioned how much of this play made any difference to my son. Might he not be just as well off spending his time with Mr. Rogers, the Sesame Street gang, and all the other characters on children's TV shows?

"Mommy," Josiah cried again, breaking into my thoughts,

"let's go to the park!"

I looked down into his eager face and, with a sigh, said, "Okay." I tossed the remaining laundry onto his bed to deal with later.

When I reached the bottom of the main stairs in our house, I found my most battered and stained tennis shoes—the ones I typically wore outside with Josiah—neatly set before me. "You got my shoes!" I said to Josiah, surprised. "Thank you."

He beamed with pride and, in that strange way three-year-olds have of reiterating their own good deeds, said, "I got your play shoes!"

Play shoes. His words struck me. I had never referred to my old battered tennis shoes as "play shoes" before. But somehow, in all our trips to the park and play in our backyard and around town, my old battered shoes had been transformed in my son's mind into "play shoes." Suddenly I realized that all the time I had spent playing with Josiah was not without value after all.

Years later, I still struggle with finding the balance between work and play, but I draw comfort from knowing that I am a mom blessed enough to own play shoes.

—*Ronica Stromberg*

Part Eight
HUMOR SHOWN IN LIFE'S SITUATIONS

Coping with our busy lives, we often find ourselves stressed out and uptight. We need to learn how to relax and not take ourselves so seriously. One way to lighten any situation is to find humor in it and laugh. This has been proven to be healthy for our bodies as well as our minds. It also strengthens relationships with our family members and friends. Laughter draws people together. It truly is the best medicine.

A joyful heart is good medicine,
but a broken spirit dries up the bones.

—PROVERBS 17:22

I thought to myself, *If I have to answer one more insignificant question, wipe one more runny nose, or bandage one more boo-boo today, I'm going to pull out my hair—and maybe the hair of whoever is standing close by!*

"I've had it, kids!" I said out loud. "I'm going to soak in a hot bubble bath, and I would strongly advise against any interruptions. Unless someone is dead or dying, do not knock on this door!"

As I eased down into my vanilla-scented bubbles, I prayed, "God, is this really what I'm supposed to be doing? I mean, don't you have something really important for me that requires a little more skill than tying shoes and cutting the crust off sandwiches?"

I hadn't always bordered on the brink of insanity. It wasn't too awfully long ago that I really had it all together. I successfully managed a booming business, counseled others in organizational skills, and drove a pretty cool automobile—one that would not seat an entire soccer team and me comfortably.

I enjoyed television shows that were not hosted by singing vegetables or a purple dinosaur. I never found the milk sitting in the pantry, and I never experienced the sheer panic of trying to remember who I was calling on the telephone before the voice at the other end could say "Hello?"

Yesterday I placed an order by phone. When the saleslady asked me for my address, I had to put her on hold. I honestly could not recall my own address! It did finally come to me, but only as I was reaching for the phone book to look it up.

What happened to cause me to end up this way, you ask? The stick turned blue. I traded in Victoria's Secret for the stretchy comfort of Hanes Her Way. Now I've boxed up all my contemporary Christian music. You'll find me rockin' instead to "Silly Songs with Larry." Yep, it's good-bye *20/20* and hello Elmo.

Sometimes I feel as though just getting dressed and making it through the day is all I ever accomplish. "Isn't there something more that you wanted me to do today, Lord?"

Finally I hear that still, small voice as I soak in my tub. God gently reminds me of what I did accomplish today. I had the privilege of listening to the hopes and dreams of a handsome young man who thinks I'm the greatest woman in the world. He stands just over three feet tall and only gets really excited over Legos and pizza, but he is funny, charming, and never boring.

I also got to see a precious smile illuminate the sweet face of my five-year-old daughter as I took time out to invade Barbie's house with green aliens. As she squealed with delight, my heart melted.

I read a couple of great classics—out loud. Move over Dickens, we have moved on to the works of Dr. Seuss. I was also able to dust, organize, clean, counsel, and cook. I kissed away the boo-boos and washed away the tears. I praised, rebuked, encouraged, and hugged—all before noon. My greatest accomplishment today included nurturing the two precious children that God has entrusted to my care.

Now my greatest challenge today—and every day—is raising these two precious children in the ways of the Lord. God does have an important job for me, and it does require great skill. It is my calling, my priority, my struggle, and my goal. I will rise to the occasion and accept the task at hand. I will love, nurture, and train my children the way God has called me to do.

When I pause for a moment, I am reminded of the awesome responsibility God has given me. Being a mom is more than being a cook, chauffeur, maid, counselor, doctor, referee, and disciplinarian (just to name a few). It's molding character, building confidence, nurturing, training, and guiding. There is no calling as consuming, challenging, and rewarding. And there is no calling as worthy of our efforts than the high calling of motherhood.

—*Ginger Plowman*

Cleaning your house while your kids are still growing is like shoveling the walk before it quits snowing.

—PHYLLIS DILLER

"Buy" THE BOOK

Throughout our parenting years, my husband and I read everything we could get our hands on—popular baby magazines, church literature, pediatrician pamphlets, Dr. Spock. We were determined to parent "by the book."

And we accepted all the expert advice we read. We sterilized. We purchased safety-tested, doctor-recommended car seats, and we locked away dangerous cleaning solvents. We studied each new stage as our child grew: the terrible twos, puberty, adolescence . . . until we reached a new stage: teenager.

Then our teen discovered cars.

"Don't worry," my husband comforted. "I read an article called 'Parenting Teenagers,' and it said you really should let your child earn the money for his first vehicle. Trust me, it will be years and years before Kyle can afford anything."

Meanwhile, Kyle was doing his own reading: the Blue Book and the classified ads. And my husband was wrong. It didn't take years and years for Kyle to afford something, because he found a "bargain." A used Jeep. His dream car.

The vehicle was a bargain because it was owned previously by another teenage boy who obviously never read anything about car ownership—especially the part about not driving your Jeep without putting any oil in it. But with check in hand, Kyle raced out to make his purchase. Then he promptly towed it home.

Have you ever really looked at a twenty-five-year-old Jeep? Up close? I'm telling you, it was put together with zippers and snaps. I've seen Matchbox cars that looked sturdier. Had I known exactly what Kyle wanted, I would have offered to *sew* him a vehicle. How could I ever trust the safety of my once securely-seatbelted child to such a flimsy vehicle? It was a good decade older than he was, and it didn't even run!

And Kyle, who had never even changed a spark plug, was going to install an entire engine in this thing?

"Don't worry," my husband reassured. "The owner's manual came with the Jeep. We'll let him study it and tinker with it awhile. He'll never be able to take it to college. It will be ages and ages before his Jeep is roadworthy."

With bad weather settling in, the Jeep was shoved into the garage—my stall, of course—where it took up residence for the entire winter.

Meanwhile, Kyle rolled up his shirt-sleeves and began dismantling. If it was loose, he wiggled it off. If it had pieces, he separated them. If it could be removed, he disassembled it. We were reminded of his Lego years. Only now the pieces were bigger. Costlier. Greasier.

Soon, the Jeep bled onto the other side of the garage (his dad's stall this time). My husband was right. It had been ages and ages, and still the Jeep wasn't running.

"Don't worry," Kyle soothed. "I'll just hoist in this rebuilt engine, and you'll have your garage back in no time."

Then he consulted experts of his own. Strange boys in dirty sneakers and sweaty T-shirts huddled over the Jeep. Parts catalogs, engine diagrams, and wiring manuals littered the kitchen counter. Margarine tubs housed Jeep entrails. And there were peculiar odors, loud noises, and greasy fingerprints—everywhere.

Meanwhile, I consulted a how-to book of my own—on stain removal. Did you know that teenage boys leave grease on everything? Refrigerator doors, milk jugs, showers and sinks, light switch plates, ceilings, and toilet lids. This job was bigger than baby wipes. I unlocked every cleaning solvent we owned. I tried everything. Some things worked better than others.

It was a long winter.

But wonder of wonders, one fine spring day that slumbering Jeep stretched and yawned, grumbled a little, then rolled from its winter bed. We held our breath when—after several false starts—Kyle coaxed it from hibernation.

We heaved a joyous sigh of relief. At last, the end of a stage. The Jeep was out and running, the house grease-free, and the garage once again our own. Now Kyle was ready to leave the safety of our home for college, driving a twenty-five-year-old vehicle with a carburetor that hiccupped and an engine that stuttered when it was running!

And run we did—to the nearest bookstore. We needed to buy a new manual, for a new stage: *How to Survive an Empty Nest.*

—*Carol McAdoo Rehme*

Parenthood remains the greatest single preserve of the amateur.

—ALVIN TOFFLER

The Lost
KEYS

"Come on, let's go," I prodded my seven-year-old son as he tugged on his socks and shoes and struggled to tie the laces. "Why can't you leave your socks and shoes on?" I asked.

"I don't know," Robbie mumbled.

I sighed. "I don't know why either," I said, exasperation filling my voice. I glanced at my watch, realizing I was late again. I was supposed to have picked up my daughter twenty minutes earlier. She had learned from experience that Mom was rarely on time, but I knew she would still worry when I wasn't there.

Still grumbling at Robbie, I threw some things in the back end of the station wagon. Suddenly it hit me. "Oh, no," I groaned. "I don't have my keys!"

Robbie rolled his eyes. This was nothing new. He was always hunting for my lost keys. "What am I going to do now? We're also locked out of the house!" I complained.

Robbie knew what to do. He ran to the next-door neighbor for our extra house key.

"I don't think she's home," I called after him. Then I ran down the driveway, hoping our back door had been left open.

A few minutes later Robbie came back. "It's okay, Mom. She's home. I've got the key," he yelled.

Unlocking the front door, Robbie and I searched through the house for my lost car keys. *Am I going to have to give my neighbor a spare car key, too?* Mentally I kicked myself for carelessly losing my keys—again.

As the minutes ticked away, I became more and more frustrated.

The keys weren't to be found anywhere. Twice I climbed the stairs and checked in my office. I looked everywhere else I thought they could possibly be at least three times. I even checked where they *couldn't* possibly be, remembering some of the strange places I had found them on occasion—under a sofa cushion, on the floor behind the television, in a beach towel. One morning I had hollered at the children for losing my keys. Where did they turn up? In my purse! I felt so foolish when the kids broke into fits of laughter.

But this isn't funny, I told myself as I glanced again at my watch. On the hunch that maybe—just maybe!—they were again in my purse, I ran back out to the car. I dumped the contents of my purse, but no keys.

I wanted to scream as I reached up and slammed the station wagon hatch shut. Suddenly I gasped.

There were my keys, hanging from the lock!

"I don't believe it," I said as Robbie and I scrambled into the car. "How could I forget that I used my keys to open the back?"

"Oh, Mom, what a silly thing to do." Robbie giggled.

"It isn't funny," I said through clenched teeth. But his laughter was infectious and I chuckled, too.

The more I laughed, the more my anger disappeared. We were still laughing when we picked up Debbie. She was annoyed by my lateness but began to giggle when she heard what I had done.

Hours later my sides still ached from laughing so hard, but I felt good. I realized I had found more than just my lost keys.

I had also found my sense of humor, which gets lost far too often in the midst of daily pressures and annoyances.

Now when I begin to get uptight or start to yell at the kids for something they have done, I remember my lost keys.

—*Marlene Bagnull*

You don't stop laughing because you grow old; you grow old because you stop laughing.

—MICHAEL PRITCHARD

Part Nine
KEEPING PRIORITIES IN ORDER

Our lives often become cluttered, causing us stress. We buy boxes, cartons, and file folders to organize all our stuff. Sometimes the importance of our personal possessions becomes blown out of proportion. Schedules, too, can become cumbersome, overflowing with activities—some of which could easily be eliminated. We need to learn to evaluate, eliminate, delegate, and simplify. We need to stop trying to be supermoms. We need to set our priorities by placing God first and our families second, but leaving time to nurture ourselves, too.

"You shall love the Lord your God with all your heart, with all your soul, and with all your mind." This is the greatest and most important commandment. The second is like it: "You shall love your neighbor as yourself."

—MATTHEW 22:37-39

A Perfect Day
FOR SLEDDING

While we try to teach our children all about life, our children teach us what life is all about.

—ANGELA SCHWINDT

"Mom, will you take us sledding?" asked eight-year-old Richard as he ran into the kitchen with his younger brother, Mike, following closely behind. "Will ya, huh?"

"Please, Mom? Pretty please?" Mike chimed in, looking up at me with irresistible blue eyes.

"Sounds like fun, boys, but I promised to bake a cake for tomorrow's church social," I said as I pointed to the cake bowl I was stirring.

"Oh, Mom, you're always doing something," Richard complained with a sigh. He turned around and motioned to his brother, "Come on, Mike, let's go upstairs. We'll 'pretend' we're sledding."

After the boys had gone up to Richard's room, I continued stirring the cake batter, but I couldn't help feeling a pang of guilt for not taking them sledding.

Putting the batter aside, I went upstairs to check on the boys. As I stood in the hallway, I overheard them talking.

"Why does Mom always have to do all that stuff for church?" Mike asked his brother, whom he considered to be much wiser because Richard was two years older.

"I guess the people at church are more important than we are."

I hadn't looked at myself through the eyes of my two young sons before. I had taught them to love God, to put Him first, and to do kind things for others. Yet how many times had I turned down one of their requests because I needed to bake or make something for people I didn't even know? I was doing things for others at the expense of my own children.

As I pondered these thoughts, God opened my eyes and I realized that I needed to put my priorities in order. I knocked on the bedroom door.

"Yeah, Mom?" Richard said, trying to sound cheerful. Apparently the boys had resigned themselves to staying home.

I walked in and sat on the bed between my two boys. "You know, guys, I've been thinking. I bet we'd have time to go sledding for an hour or two."

"Yippee!" shouted Mike, bouncing up and down on the bed.

Richard studied me for a moment and asked, "What about the cake you promised to bake for the church people?"

"Richard, that's important, but not as important as you guys are. I can bake that cake after dinner, and no one at the church will ever know the difference."

Mike looked at me wide-eyed. "Do they care when you bake a cake?"

Richard answered. "No, silly, she just means she has to get it to the church on time. Come on, let's go sledding!"

The boys raced downstairs to the coat closet, giggling as they pulled on their parkas, boots, and mittens.

As we walked out into the cold winter air, a warmth inside assured me I had made the right decision. Right now my number one priority was a sledding date with my two boys.

I looked across the highway at the nearby hill and said, "It's a perfect day for sledding, boys."

—*Susan Titus Osborn*

The Day
THE DOORS CLOSED

"I'll be home this afternoon, and we'll do something together then, okay?" I yelled to my eight-year-old daughter as I hurried out the door. It was one of those months when I was running full-speed, speaking every weekend, staying up late at night to write, getting by with as little housework and parenting as I could in order to meet my deadlines and obligations.

I didn't think again about that promise I made to Dana until I pulled into my driveway at the end of the day and saw the sign—hand-scrawled in green marker—that was taped onto the garage door: "Welcome Home, Mommy!"

I smiled, realizing that Dana had missed me while I was gone.

As I walked into the house, I expected her to pop out from the other end of the door. But instead, the house was strangely quiet. "Hello . . . " I called. "Mom's home." I walked up the stairs, headed toward my study where I would put down my bags, sort through the papers and messages, and get everything unpacked before I could relax and really "be at home."

But neither my husband nor my daughter met me on the way upstairs. Instead, as I rounded the top of the stairs I noticed my study door was shut, and taped to it was another sign scrawled in green marker: "No study today. Too much hard work!"

I turned around and headed to my bedroom where I heard the television. But that door was shut as well. Taped to it was a colorful sign that stopped me in my tracks: "I love you, Mommy! I love your Chicken Enchiladas! (Someone had been scolded a few nights earlier for not being grateful for enchiladas.) I love your hair, smile, clothes, face, and eyes! Love, Dana Katherine McMenamin."

At that moment I felt a presence. I turned and saw my Dana, with her arms and legs blocking the door of my study, eyes open wide with anticipation, and a mischievous smile on her face as if to say, *Do you notice me now? Will you play with me now?*

I dropped my bags onto the floor, walked over to Dana, and knelt down. Hugging her tightly, I whispered into her ear, "Thank you. It means so much to know that you want to spend time with me. I'm just so sorry you had to shut all the doors in front of me to get me to stop and notice you. The rest of the day is just ours, okay?"

Her smile told me that was the right response.

I never did open the door to my study that evening. I just left my bags right there in the hallway. And Dana and I went downstairs and played a favorite game of hers—over and over again. Then we cuddled up on the couch and watched a favorite movie of hers—one we had already seen over and over again. For the first time in a long while, I took the time to just be with her.

The pace of my life has changed dramatically since the day that Dana closed those doors. And now I live by this motto: If God opens certain doors, I'll walk through them into the opportunities He has for me. But if they're left shut, I'll just stay home and be with Dana. After all, if I'm too busy to notice the ones in life I love the most, I'm definitely too busy to realize who and what is most important.

—*Cindi McMenamin*

We all find time to do what we really want to do.

—WILLIAM FEATHER

Six Rose Hips, Two Bobby Pins,
AND A BALL OF BLUE STRING

Dost thou love life? Then do not squander time, for that is the stuff life is made of.

—BENJAMIN FRANKLIN

One crisp, spring Saturday morning my eight-year-old daughter snuck up behind me as I stood knee-deep in mounds of dirty laundry that had accumulated during the past week.

"Take us to the park, Mom," begged Erin, as she reached into her pocket and pulled out the incentive. "Look at what I'll give you if you'll take us." She opened her hand, and resting on her palm for the taking were three pennies, a fishing bobber, and one smooth piece of shiny white shell.

"That's tempting, Erin," I explained, "but I have a lot of work to do today. Look at all this laundry. I'll never get it done! Plus, we have to grocery shop, and Dad wants us to rake the lawn." I took a long, deep breath of exhaustion, caused simply from thinking about all that had to be done.

Then I looked at my daughter who needed my attention after her own busy week of schoolwork, and I said, "Let's wait and see how much work I get accomplished, and we'll take it from there. If I didn't have to work during the week, I could have all this stuff done and have more time for you."

Erin turned and bounded away contentedly (or so I thought). But within minutes she was back. "Mom, look," she continued, "if you promise to take us to the park today, I'll give you all this." Erin again reached into her pockets, and this time laid each item delicately on our washing machine for display.

I eagerly looked at each new incentive: six rose hips, one silver washer, a small ball of blue string, two bobby pins, one rose petal, one piece of chipped blacktop from our driveway, and a red piece of broken brick.

"Wow, Erin," I exclaimed, "you mean if I promise to take you to the park, you'd give me all this?"

"That's right, Mom," she answered, "it's really a good deal."

"Well . . . " I continued, "I think I'd feel guilty taking all of this just for taking you to the park. I'd feel like I got the better end of the deal. What do you think?"

"You're right, Mom," she answered, "this is an awful lot of stuff. Why don't you just take the six rose hips, the two bobby pins, and the ball of blue string, and we'll call it even."

As Erin tugged at my heartstrings, I knew I had to reevaluate my priorities. *What's more important,* I thought, *time with my children, or having clean laundry?* I knew it was my kids, hands down!

"You've got a deal," I answered. "We'll leave for the park in an hour."

Erin smiled with satisfaction. "Thanks, Mom. I love you!"

Tell me, how could a mom say no?

—*Wendy Dunham*

Part Ten
GOD'S STILL, SMALL VOICE

In order to listen to God, we need to slow down our frantic pace. We need to be still in order to hear His voice. God often speaks softly to us, and we miss what He is saying if we're running around in a frenzy or talking all the time. Even Jesus, when He was here on earth, went off by Himself to spend quiet time, listening to His Father's voice. If we follow His example, we too will hear God's still, small voice.

After dismissing the crowds, He went up on the mountain by Himself to pray. When evening came, He was there alone.

—MATTHEW 14:23

Lessons
FROM CHAZ

The day started out like any other day as I fixed breakfast for my two-year-old son, Chaz, and his baby sister, Harley. Chaz was sitting at the dining room table waiting patiently for his bowl of cereal, and I was in the kitchen mixing Harley's formula and preparing her oatmeal. My mind had already wandered to the tasks ahead of me that day. The laundry was piling up, and the floor really needed to be swept.

"Mommy?" Chaz called.

I continued what I was doing and didn't respond. After two years of parenthood, I was beginning to understand why so many mothers unconsciously ignore their children. I didn't mean to ignore him, but at that particular moment my thoughts were elsewhere.

"Mommy?" Chaz tried again. When I didn't respond within a few seconds, my two-year-old showed his age and shouted, "Mommy!"

When my son's voice finally broke into my thoughts, I turned to him. "What?!" I snapped.

"I want some milk, pleeeeeeease."

"Oh, okay," I said, feeling a little guilty about snapping at him. After all, it wasn't his fault that I didn't acknowledge him until he shouted.

The morning continued as normal until later in the day when I was trying to get my son's attention. I had his lunch ready for him, and he was busy playing with his toy kitchen.

"Chaz," I said.

106

The little boy continued to "cook" with his pots and pans.

"Chaz," I said again, this time raising my voice a little. "Chaz!" I finally shouted.

He turned to me, and in a disgusted voice snapped, "What?!"

Is that my two-year-old? I thought.

The Lord spoke to my heart in that moment, and it was almost as if I could hear Him say, "No, that's you."

Oh, the lessons I learned that day from Chaz! Before that moment, I hadn't completely realized what an impact my words and actions had on my children's lives. The thought scared me a little. Even at the age of two, Chaz was already picking up my attitude. That fact made me understand that my attitude needed work. Things I said and the way I behaved didn't seem so bad until I saw them reflected in Chaz.

Then the Lord brought one final thought to mind. Do I make Him have to shout at me before I acknowledge Him? Sadly, I had to answer yes. Sometimes I make the Lord shout at me rather than listening for His still, small voice. How many times had I missed His gentle nudging and forced Him to shout? Could I have avoided unnecessary pain if I'd only been more in tune to God's voice?

"I've got some work to do," I admitted, even though I knew Chaz didn't know what I meant.

"What?"

"Your lunch is ready," I said, helping him into his chair. As we sat down I said a prayer of thanks for the food. I also thanked the Lord for teaching me some valuable lessons through Chaz, and I purposed in my heart to implement those lessons in my life.

—*Crystal Ratcliff*

Once I put effort into my listening and fine-tuned the ears of my spirit, I began to hear God.

—LORRAINE PINTUS

The Forgotten
MATH BOOK

I had just settled down to a major writing project when the phone rang.

"Mom, I forgot my math book!" My teenage daughter's voice sounded anxious on the other end of the line.

"Oh, no!" I mumbled, annoyed at the interruption.

"I'm really sorry, Mom," Lia said.

I took a deep breath to control my rising impatience. "I'll bring it out to you, honey, but meet me at the front door of the school, because I'm busy and don't have time to come in."

I grabbed Lia's math book from the kitchen counter and rushed out the door.

Am I doing the right thing? I wondered as I backed the car out of the driveway. Lately, whenever Lia got into a jam I bailed her out. If she missed the school bus because she had gotten up late, I drove her to school. If she forgot her lunch, I took it to her. If a heavy homework load kept her from doing her chores, I did them for her.

Artistically inclined, Lia was not an irresponsible person, just absent-minded sometimes. Yet the questions bombarded my mind: *Was I really helping my daughter, or was I simply encouraging the development of a bad trait? Should I make her suffer the consequences of her actions, or should I be understanding? Where should I draw the line between justice and mercy?*

As I drove the ten miles to Lia's school, I complained to God. "How am I ever going to meet my deadlines with yet another interruption?"

Then I heard God's still, small voice in my mind. *Do you remember the time you ran out of gas because you forgot to fill the tank, and I sent a policeman to help you?*

I shifted in the driver's seat. "Yes, Lord," I replied.

And do you remember the time you carelessly hit a curb and ruptured a tire on the way to a speaking engagement?

"Yes, Lord," I said, my cheeks growing hot with conviction.

How well I remembered that incident! Having gone to a nearby grocery store to phone for help, I unexpectedly met a friend who graciously drove me to my destination in time for me to speak. If God had been so merciful to me in my hour of need, how could I be anything less to my daughter?

"Okay, Lord, I get the message," I said as I pulled up into the school driveway. "Please forgive me."

I got out of the car and watched as Lia shuffled toward me.

"Mom, I'm so sorry," she said with downcast eyes.

I lifted her chin and looked deep into her stunning brown eyes.

"Honey," I said, "I'm the one who should be sorry for being so impatient with you. Will you forgive me?"

"Sure, Mom," she said.

"You know," I continued, placing a kiss on her nose, "I'm so glad I have you to bring your math book to."

Her face lit up with the beautiful smile I'd grown to love so well.

"Thanks, Mom," she said. "I'm glad I have you, too."

And I'm glad I have You, Lord, I thought silently as I handed Lia her book.

—*Mary Ann Diorio*

Who will not mercy unto others show,
How can he mercy ever hope to have?

—EDMUND SPENSER

Jesus
Loves You!

"Mom! I can't reach them!"

My four-year-old daughter, Caitlyn, was dangling over the edge of the shopping cart trying to reach inside. I sighed and handed her a tube of toothpaste and a package of toilet paper to put on the conveyor belt.

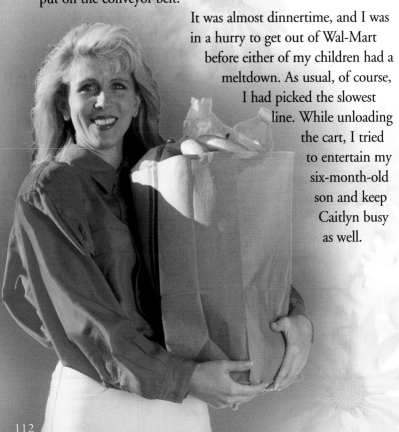

It was almost dinnertime, and I was in a hurry to get out of Wal-Mart before either of my children had a meltdown. As usual, of course, I had picked the slowest line. While unloading the cart, I tried to entertain my six-month-old son and keep Caitlyn busy as well.

The conveyor belt was soon full, and I grew a bit irritated at the clerk who was busily chatting with the customer ahead of me instead of ringing up her purchases.

"I don't know why they keep having more babies," the clerk said loudly, smacking her gum. "They should just send 'em back." She laughed loudly. Her nametag said *Rhonda*.

I scowled as I purposely looked away from the clerk. *Can't she see I have two children?* I looked at my precious babies, both of whom had difficult journeys into the world. I knew because of medical reasons that I couldn't have any more.

Rhonda finally noticed me standing there. "Oh, here I am opening my big mouth when she's got two of 'em," she said to the lady in front of me. Then she laughed again.

She advanced the conveyor belt, removed the separator bar, and started ringing up my purchases on the other lady's bill.

"No, that's mine."

She kept on adding my things to the bag.

"That's mine!" I shouted, the irritation showing in my voice.

"Huh?" Rhonda grunted, finally looking in my direction.

"Those are my things in that bag."

"Oh—" Then she used my Savior's name in vain.

I gritted my teeth and rolled my eyes. I hated how cavalierly people used Jesus' name. To me, she was doing the equivalent of swearing.

Caitlyn was hanging on the front of the cart. I hoped she hadn't heard Rhonda's words. But it was obvious she had. Her eyes lit up, and she smiled at the clerk. "Jesus loves you!"

113

"What's that?" Rhonda glanced at her distractedly.

"Jesus loves you!"

"Uh, yeah." She busied herself straightening out the bags.

My heart swelled with pride. My daughter wasn't afraid to tell a stranger the greatest news of all: *Jesus loves you.* Yet I felt a bit admonished by my daughter. She heard someone say Jesus' name and instantly linked that with His love.

Me? I was so consumed with my own irritation at Rhonda's rudeness and being delayed that it didn't occur to me that Jesus loved her, too. That day at Wal-Mart, I heard God's voice through my four-year-old's words, "Jesus loves you."

—*Jennifer Tiszai*

The soul is healed by being with children.

—FYODOR DOSTOEVSKY

Contributors

Marlene Bagnull and her husband, Paul, are the parents of three grown children. She directs the Colorado and Greater Philadelphia Christian Writers Conferences and is the author of eight books including *My Turn to Care: Encouragement for Caregivers of Aging Parents*.

Cindy Barber now enjoys being a stay-at-home mom after working for twelve years in the advertising business. Cindy, her husband, and their three children live in Atlanta, Georgia. You may contact her at <u>rughbarber@bellsouth.net</u>.

Dr. Mary Ann Diorio is a widely published author and professional speaker. She is founder and director of "Life Coaching for Professionals." Mary Ann and her husband are the parents of two grown daughters and reside in Millville, New Jersey.

Dr. Rebecca Dowden is a professor, counselor, author, and speaker. Rebecca and her husband are the founders of "Abounding Love Ministries," which offers counseling and workshops for couples. Rebecca resides in Houston, Texas, with her husband and son.

Wendy Dunham is a wife, mom, inspirational writer, and registered therapist for differently-abled children. When she's not playing with her children, gardening, or doing laundry, she can be found at her computer, writing. Contact her at 3148 Lake Road, Brockport, New York 14420 or call 716-637-0535.

Dena Dyer is a writer and speaker with credits in over 100 magazines, such as *Woman's World, Today's Christian Woman,* and *Discipleship Journal.* She has contributed to several books, including *God's Little Devotional Book for Grandparents.* For more information, visit www.denadyer.com.

Deb Haggerty is an author and speaker living in Orlando, Florida, with her husband, Roy, and "Cocoa the Dog." Jimmy, now known as James, lives and works in Jacksonville, Florida. Contact Deb at 407-856-2897 or toll-free 1-888-332-7757. Or write her at 9725 Blandford Road, Orlando, Florida 32827-7039. Her email is Deb@DebHaggerty.com.

Bonnie Compton Hanson is author of the *Ponytail Girls* book series for girls plus other books, poems, stories, and articles (including stories in three *Chicken Soup* books). Contact her at 3330 South Lowell Street, Santa Ana, California 92707 or call 714-751-7824. Her email is bonnieh1@worldnet.att.net.

Kathy Ide lives in Southern California with her husband, Richard, and two sons, Mike and Tom ("Tommy," who is now in his late twenties). She is a full-time freelance author, editor, and proofreader. Her website is www.KathyIde.com. Email her at kathy@kathyide.com.

Cindi McMenamin is a national speaker and freelance writer who is the author of *Heart Hunger* and *When Women Walk Alone.* She lives with her family in Southern California. For more information on her ministry, see her website at www.cindispeaks.com.

Janet Lynn Mitchell is a wife and mother of three. She is also an inspirational speaker and author of numerous articles and stories in compilations. Janet's latest book, *A Special Kind of Love*, coauthored by Susan Osborn, will be available in 2004. Janet can be reached at Janetlm@prodigy.net or by faxing to 714-633-6309.

Karen O'Connor is an award-winning author of thirty-eight books, a retreat speaker, and a writing instructor. Her most recent book, *Help, Lord, I'm Having a Senior Moment: Notes to God on Growing Older*, was published by Servant Publishers in 2002.

Susan Titus Osborn is director of the Christian Communicator Manuscript Critique Service. She is a contributing editor of *The Christian Communicator* magazine and an adjunct professor. She has authored twenty-five books. Susan and Dick, her husband, have a blended family of five children and ten grandchildren. Contact Susan at Susanosb@aol.com.

Ginger Plowman, wife and mother of two, is the author of *Wise Words for Moms* and the founder of "Preparing the Way Ministry," for which she speaks coast-to-coast on biblical parenting. Visit her website at www.gingerplowman.com.

Crystal Ratcliff and her husband, Marc, reside in Kansas. They have two children: Chaz is two and Harley is one. Crystal is a stay-at-home mom and runs her own business as a Stampin' Up!®

demonstrator. She is also the author of an inspirational novel entitled *Trials of Faith*.

Carol McAdoo Rehme, mother of four, feathers her now-empty nest with a "second" career as author, speaker, and storyteller. She is executive director of "Vintage Voices, Inc.," a non-profit organization dedicated to providing programming for eldercare facilities. Contact her at carol@rehme.com, www.rehme.com, or 970-669-5791.

Rhonda Rhea is a humor columnist and feature writer for Christian publications throughout the U.S. and Canada. Her latest book is *Amusing Grace*, published by Cook Communications. She is also a popular conference speaker. Visit her website at www.rhondarhea.net.

Tamara Rice is a youth pastor's wife and busy mother of two preschoolers. She enjoys doing freelance editing and writing in her spare time (i.e. naptime!). Raised on the mission field of Bangladesh, she now lives in Southern California.

Judith Scharfenberg is wife to Richard, mother of six, grand-mother of eight, and a retired children's librarian, as well as an active author, speaker, and discipler. Her passion is encouraging everyone to put Jesus first in all they do. She says, "Being a wife and mom are the best jobs on earth."

Dayle Allen Shockley's articles have appeared in dozens of publications. She is a regular contributor to *The Dallas Morning News* and a contributing columnist at www.Homebodies.org and www.NewsAndOpinion.com. Dayle is the author of three books and is a writing instructor at a Houston college.

Judy Ann Squier has learned firsthand about God's power made perfect in weakness. Born without legs, she has lived life to the fullest. She has been married thirty-three years to David and is the mother of three grown daughters: Emily, Elizabeth and Naphtalie. She is also a speaker and author who writes travel articles for the disabled.

Ronica Stromberg is the author of the children's novel, *The Glass Inheritance*, published in 2001 by Royal Fireworks Press, as well as numerous short stories in nonfiction books and magazines. As the mother of two boys, she has learned to value her play shoes.

Jennifer Tiszai is a wife and mother of two young children in Southern California. She writes devotionals, small-group Bible studies, and website articles for one of the largest churches in the nation. She is currently working on her first novel.